Self-regulation through poetry

Sueda Abouzanad

BookLeaf Publishing

Presentation by *BookLeaf Publishing*

Web: www.bookleafpub.com

E-mail: info@bookleafpub.com

ISBN: 9789357211550

First edition 2023

ACKNOWLEDGEMENT

To those that listened to my countless drafts and believed in me, I thank you.

To those that inspired some of these poems, I guess there was a reason.

Welcome

Welcome,

Welcome to the world…

At birth we are welcomed with our name

Those letters, lay our foundation,

Our first affiliation.

Welcome to your first day at school…

Happy faces beam down,

Nervous teary eyes look around,

Years past by, Knowledge grows, life happens,
friendships are formed and broken,

Education, a token,

Of time served,

Well preserved,

Presented to you, tightly curled, under the entrance of a new sign.

Welcome to the Real World…

Eager? Happy? Stressed?

It greets all,

With no time to stall,

Thoughts are put into action,

You handle all kinds of interaction,

In time, You welcome others into Your world,

Welcome…

friends, family, partners, children, and pets,

Huddled under your umbrella, they see you,

Through the highs and the lows,

Through, growth, healing, and love,

They watch you rise above,

They watch you dive below,

They watch you fight the tide,

Inside.

Only to resurface and remain grounded,

forever, unbounded.

Welcomed,

Anew.

Soul sisters

Friends like we,

were always destined to be.

Written in the stars,

before earth or mars,

the first constellation,

dreamed into creation.

Our souls cosmically connected,

specifically selected,

to withstand the tests of time.

While remaining, Forevermore,

Partners In Crime.

Life is a Broadway act

I watch life through a screen, my body the set,
the play.

my Face the Actor,

my Mouth the Star,

my Eyes, glossy windows, to the sorrow within.

This façade is tiring,

All actors need breaks.

In come the bathroom excuses, the I'll be backs,

The door closes, the curtains come down,

Tears escape and run down,

Time moves slowly,

I get up, look at the mirror, wipe away the rain,
evidence of my internal pain,

Smile, the mask is back on, the actors are back,

The star is on stage, Ready,

The door opens,

The curtain lifts,

Showtime.

Egg Shells

I'm tired of walking on eggshells,

jumping from rock to rock,

I'm over watching what I say,

can't be bothered to beat around the bush,

my voice always being shushed.

Not wanting to offend,

my boundaries always being bent,

I'm tired of rewording my sentences,

I no longer think you deserve that grace,

especially while you continue to stomp so
loudly,
in My space.

Not everyone deserves your love

Is it wrong to care?

To have your heart laid out so bare.

In a world where love seems strained, fading,

the expression of love itself so stunted,

That it only remains that…
an expression.

Not a plausible possession.

I expressed my love for you,

my deep admiration and respect for you,

I shared it with you so freely,

I wore my heart on my sleeve,
for you.

Only for it to be beaten and bruised and then left broken,

by the words you and yours had spoken.

Your words were not just words,

they were sharp-beaked birds.

Aiming straight into my heart,

bulls' eye,
dart.

Why is my freedom to love, to care, so
threatening?

In this world where the darkness is beckoning,

I will not stop and succumb to these ill-fated
wishes,

I will not give up,

They cannot break me,

And so, they cannot make me,

I Will Not Give Up My Freedom to Care.

To all those that said, “You’re too much”.

I’ve spent too many years wishing I was
someone else,

a colder, meaner, more distant, version of me.

I cursed and cried at my warm heart,

even still it kept up its beat,

Cheering me on,
giving me time to realise,

It wasn’t me; it was You,

who needed to change.

Yearning

Empty arms,
swing side to side, gently,
Silence seeks the lullabies notes
Ready to be sung,
Yearning,
for You.

Anne

Looking back, I feel so blessed,
you were always so impressed,

I'm lucky God entrusted me with you,
God knew no one else would do,

sure, there are some things I would do
differently,

When it's my turn,

But who am I to know, what's it like being you
You've always been there when we have felt
blue,

A shoulder to lean on,

A warm hug,

A comforting ear,

I hold you so dear,

I hope I can be,
half the Anne,
you are to me

Chosen family

If I had to do this all over,

all the trials and tribulations,

I would do it all again,

If it meant choosing you all,

And being chosen by you all
Again.

Kings 123

A dreamy eyed girl; an academic whirl, a
hopeful student,

She sat in class, with a flask, full of liquid gold,
She was bold, we were told, and she had a
dream to behold.

She sat her exams; the first time, so full of the
jitter,
However, her results were bitter, but she was not
a quitter,

She retook the year, her future before her, kings
was on the horizon,

Fast-forward the second time; she had a
mountain to climb, as fate had hit her again,

The girl; Khan, was distraught, she could be
bought, there was no one she hadn't fought.

Kings One Two,

She thought a few, and hope began to brew,

She'd try again, the last stand against the land,

A new route, that wouldn't lead to the boot, a
journey to Kings One Two Three.

Bring the brie, the tree and me,

Wear all of your things,
we are at the start of Kings 123.

You are my person

You are my person, the one whose face quickens the pace, of my heart.

Whose voice is my favourite choice of sound.

But am I yours? Used to think we were bound.
As a friendship like ours is rarely found.

Before,

Before, I thought I was your person.

The one whose face brightens and lightens your world.

Before them, before this, before you now.

I thought it was me, you brought you so much glee.

What a selfish thought I now see.

They, the new One, is your person,

Who you call first,

Message first,
Ask about,
Think about,
Want to be around

And be bound to.

Its something I'm coming to accept,

this change in status,
though I think about taking a hiatus.

I can't, not now, not ever.

I love too deeply, too completely.

A break, an ending like that? It would destroy me.

I pray,

I pray to not feel as I do,

to have the strength to not feel a love this deep,
for you.

However as much as I try and fight it, you are and will always be my person.

Even if I am no longer,

yours.

Kiss

A Kiss,

Usually given to those we'd never want to miss,

On the forehead,

The cheek,

The lips,

Sometimes as an act of emotion, given to those
we love;

Passionately,
Desperately,
Sympathetically,

The dot at the end of 'Goodbye.'

In between tears,
Paralyzed by fears,

A quick peck, given hurriedly without thought,

The exclamation mark at the end of an excited 'Hi!'

Accompanied by a handshake,

A hug,

Touch.

Haiku

Watching from the hill,

the birds play with autumns' leaves,

waiting for Winter.

Eddy

With red hair and piercing blue eyes,

she is so very wise,

with sharp wit and a dry sense of humour,

she’ll stand firm and wont let the world, around,

consume her.

Loyal to the core with a heart of gold,

we are all so lucky to have someone so bold,

she is strong, brave, and beautiful,

and I am so glad she came into my life all those,
years ago.

Words unsaid

Surrounded by your embrace,
A smile creeps upon my face,

Secrets shared in hush tones,
Gather beneath our bare bones,

Eyes sparkle with delight,
While our lips remain too polite,

To express how we truly feel,
Waiting for the other to seal the deal.

Courage gathered, you take the plunge,
I absorb your words, like a sponge,

Soaking in loves glee,
Our hearts are shipped out to sea,

Away from all the doom and gloom,
Love is free to bloom,

But, before caps have hit the ground,

To a Nine – Five we are bound,

Working hard to survive,

We barely have time to keep love alive,

The years fly by,

Work, home, kids, there's barely have time to look up at the sky,

Tears streaming down my face,

I can't believe we have gotten to this place,

Hearts disconnected,

Anger misdirected,

Words unspoken,
Broken,

Left hanging in the air,

Fill the room be both share,

How do we get back to us?

To reconnect and discuss?

I see your car pull out,

I want to scream and shout,

I wish you knew,

how much,

I still love you.

Crave

I crave a love so deep the ocean would be jealous,

I crave a love so intense, it would be considered an extreme sport,

I crave a love so real, we won't want to be anywhere else,

I crave a love so strong, separating would cause the end of times,

But most of all, I crave a love with you.

To the one I waited for

Under the cover of the night,

Beneath the sun so bright,

I prayed for you,

Head to the ground,

Tears streaming down,

I prayed for you,

Years passed by,

I thought we would never get to meet,

Then next thing I know, you're on my street,

At my door,
Black shirt, brown trousers, flowers in hand,
Vauxhall Zafira parked on the neighbour's land,

Arms wrapped tight,

I knew you were Mr Right.

Growth

Becoming a better person is hard,

no wonder songs about it were never sung by the bard,

It’s easier to remain the same,

or become someone lame,

Why should I grow?

When others only reap what I sow?

Stuck in their ways, not wanting to change,
to follow.

The World needs better,
I say,

holding on to that thought,

I apply what I’ve been taught.
by Life,

won’t let others keep me down,

leave them behind I say,

to the past they are bound,

not all change is bad,

and so, to the future I look,

where I no longer go by the book.

Spring

Perched upon the branch,

The birds tolerate winters harsh snow,

Deep in their dens,

The bears hibernate through the cold,

Nestled in their warm burrows,

Badgers sleep through the season,

All waiting,

for spring

www.ingramcontent.com/pod-product-compliance
Lightning Source LLC
Chambersburg PA
CBHW051752130826
49812CB00033B/1120
* 9 7 8 9 3 5 7 2 1 1 5 5 0 *